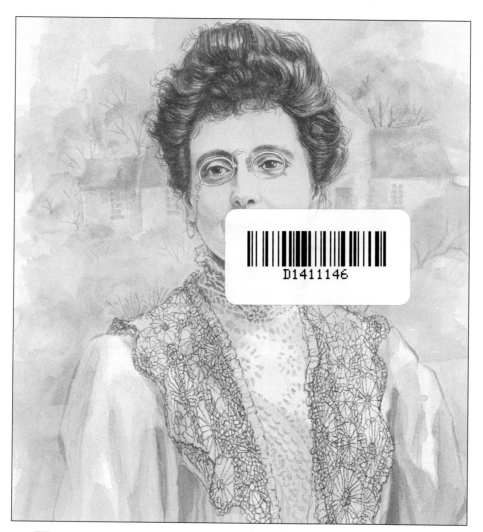

Lucy Maud Montgomery

Mollie Gillen

Fitzhenry & Whiteside Limited

Contents

THE CANADIANS
A Continuing Series

Lucy Maud Montgomery

Author: Mollie Gillen
Design: Kerry Designs
Cover Illustration: John Mardon

Canadian Cataloguing in Publication Data
Gillen, Mollie.
Lucy Maud Montgomery
(The Canadians)
Bibliography: P. 64
ISBN 1-55041-461-5

1. Montgomery, Lucy Maud, 1874-1942 – Biography. 2. Women novelists – Canada – Biography. I. Series
PS8526.045Z6152   C813'.5'2   C99-001628-6
PR9199.3.M6Z6152

© 1999 Fitzhenry & Whiteside Limited
195 Allstate Parkway, Markham, Ontario L3R 4T8

Anne

On May 2, 1907, a 33-year-old writer who signed her name L.M. *Montgomery* sat down in the little farm home of her grandparents at Cavendish, Prince Edward Island, and wrote to a pen friend, an Alberta homesteader named Ephraim Weber.

Well, last fall and winter I went to work and wrote a book. I didn't squeak a word to anyone about it because I feared desperately I wouldn't find a publisher for it. When I got it finished and typewritten I sent it to the L.C. Page Co. of Boston and a fortnight ago, after two months of suspense, I got a letter from them accepting my book and offering to publish it on the 10 per cent royalty basis.

L.M. Montgomery (known as Maud to her family and friends) had called her book "Anne of Green Gables". It was the story of an elderly brother and sister who had applied to an orphanage for a boy who, they hoped, would be able to help them on their farm. Instead of a boy, however, a lively, talkative, red-haired girl named Anne Shirley was sent to them. Miss Montgomery thought her book "wasn't half-bad," but she warned Mr. Weber, "Don't stick up your ears now, imagining that the great Canadian novel has been written at last. It is merely a juvenilish story, ostensibly for girls."

The book, published in June 1908, was unexpectedly an instant success. It was reprinted six times in the first five months. Two movies were to be made from it, as well as two television series and a popular musical. Since its first publication, millions of copies have been sold in many languages and in braille for the blind. *Anne of Green Gables* is as popular today as it was in 1908. "Anne seems to have hit the public taste," wrote Maud, delighted and surprised. But even then she could hardly realize that the simple story she had intended for girls would become a worldwide bestseller, still at the close of the century being read with pleasure by children and adults alike.

Chapter 1
Childhood

Hugh John Montgomery

The daughter who was born to Hugh John and Clara Woolner Montgomery on November 30, 1874, in the tiny village of Clifton, P.E.I., was christened Lucy Maud – Lucy for her Grandmother Macneill, and Maud for herself. Hugh was 33, his bride 21. The new baby inherited a long line of Island ancestors from both father and mother. The Macneills and Montgomerys had arrived in Prince Edward Island from Scotland about a hundred years earlier, and both families had produced people of importance in the community. William Macneill, Maud's great-grandfather, was a member of the Island legislature from 1814 to 1834. He was known as "old Speaker Macneill." Her grandfather, Donald Montgomery, was a member of the Prince Edward Island parliament for 34 years, and served for 20 more years in the Canadian Senate, to which he had been appointed in 1873. Montgomerys, Macneills, Townsends, Simpsons and Campbells still form a network of relationships across the Island, and this newest member of the clan carried some of the blood of all of them.

Maud's mother was not strong; she died when the child was only 21 months

Clara Montgomery

old. Hugh Montgomery gave his baby daughter to her mother's parents, Alexander and Lucy Macneill, to care for and raise. Alexander Macneill's farm was at the small settlement of Cavendish on the northern coast of the Island, less than a kilometre from the shore where the great Atlantic waves rolled in, and 38 kilometres from the nearest railway station. Here Maud lived and grew. She had many uncles and aunts and cousins on the Island, and the farm owned by her father's parents was only twenty kilometres away, but she did not see them very often because travel was slow by horse and buggy, and people had a lot of work to keep them busy on their farms. The men would look after the animals, plough the land, sow and reap the grain, and catch fish from the ocean. The women would keep the house clean and tidy, sew and mend clothes, bake and cook, make butter, preserve the fruit from the orchard, and tend the garden where flowers and vegetables grew.

"I spent my childhood and girlhood in an old-fashioned Cavendish farmhouse, surrounded by apple orchards," Maud wrote later. No place could have offered more to satisfy her eager appetite for beauty.

L.M. Montgomery's birthplace, New London

Alexander Macneill

Lucy Macneill

Everything was invested with a kind of fairy grace and charm, emanating from my own fancy - the trees that whispered nightly around the old house where I slept, the woodsy nooks I explored, the homestead fields...the sea whose murmur was never out of my ears...amid all the commonplaces of life I was very near to a kingdom of ideal beauty. Between it and me hung only a thin veil. I could never draw it quite aside, but sometimes a wind fluttered it and I caught a glimpse of the enchanting realm beyond – only a glimpse – but those glimpses have always made life worthwhile.

Uncle John and Aunt Annie Campbell lived at Park Corner, not far from Grandfather Montgomery. Maud loved the drive to get there, "such a pretty one, those winding thirteen miles through hill and wood, and by river and shore." But she was afraid of the drawbridges over two of the rivers that had to be crossed. Perhaps she thought the bridge might rise up when she was half-way over, and deposit the carriage, horses and passengers into the water.

The Campbell house was "a big white one, smothered in orchards," next to a shining lake, and there were three cheerful cousins to play with. Grandfather Montgomery's home was a charming old frame house "full of cupboards and nooks, and little, unexpected flights of stairs." Maud especially loved the pair of white china dogs with green spots that stood on the sitting-room mantel. Her father teased her by telling her a story she half believed – that when the clock struck midnight, the china dogs jumped down to the hearth and barked.

From her childhood she always remembered two moments of great pain. One pain was physical, when she picked up the wrong end of a red-hot poker. The other was a pain in her heart when her beloved kitten Pussy-willow was poisoned. One

dreadful day, she thought the world was going to end. She had heard her Aunt Emily read from the paper that someone believed this would happen on a certain day, and Maud was sure it must be true because it had been printed, in a newspaper. She could not understand why the grown-ups did not seem to be at all worried about it. When the day came, she lived through it in fear and trembling, and did not get over her fear until darkness fell and she realized that her beautiful world still existed, as green and lovely as ever.

The imaginative little girl had no companions of her own age to play with until she was six, when Aunt Emily took her across to the nearby schoolhouse. A year later, two little boys, Wellington and David Nelson, known as Well and Dave, came to stay for some months with the Macneills. Before this, Maud had created imaginary playmates from the shadowy

The Macneill homestead, where Maud lived and where Anne of Green Gables *was written, was "... an old-fashioned Cavendish farmhouse, surrounded by apple orchards." Unhappily, the house has since been torn down, and only the foundations now remain.*

Maud, aged six

reflections of herself in the glass doors of the book-case. Katy Maurice, she pretended, was the one who lived in the left-hand door. In the right-hand door was Lucy Gray, a grown-up, widowed lady who seemed to have lived a sad life. Many people came to the Macneill farmhouse, for Alexander Macneill was the village postmaster, and Maud probably overheard much grown-up gossip from which she concocted the sad history of Lucy Gray. She said later that she had had a lonely childhood, but there is a difference between being lonely and being solitary, and Maud Montgomery's loneliness was too full of imaginary people and incidents to have made her childhood an unhappy one.

Real-life adventures, too, sometimes came her way. When she was five, an exciting visit to Charlottetown, the capital of the Island province, became a lifelong memory. There were shop windows full of nuts and candies and oranges, and many strange sights. There was a woman shaking rugs – "On the top of a house...We shook rugs in the yard" – and there was a dim room glimpsed through an open door, full of barrels and curly wood shavings. In Charlottetown, Maud met the first of many "kindred spirits" – a black-eyed, black-haired little girl carrying a pitcher down a sidestreet. "We told each other how old we were, and how many dolls we had, and almost everything else there was to tell except our names, which neither of us thought about. When we parted, I felt as though I were leaving a lifelong friend."

With Well and Dave, Maud fished in the brooks for trout (she was very proud that she managed to put the worm on her own hook). They planted little gardens, carried breakfasts and dinners to the fishermen on the shore, built playhouses from fir boughs, gathered shells. Maud loved the trees and gave them all names: Little Syrup tree, Spotty tree, the Spider tree, the White Lady birch. The children used to sit on the porch in the twilight, when Well and Dave would tell ghost stories about fearful "white things" fluttering in the Haunted Wood. One day an all-too-real "white thing" flapped under the juniper tree and sent the three children shrieking with fear into the house. It was only a tablecloth set out to bleach in the sun and caught by the wind, but they were sure it was a ghost.

Maud could not remember a time when she was unable to read. The Macneill house was full of books; Hans Andersen's *Tales*, a two-volume *History of the World* full of coloured pictures, books of poetry – Tennyson, Whittier, Scott, Longfellow, Byron, Milton, Burns. She also found a few novels – *Rob Roy*, *The Pickwick Papers*, *Zanoni*; and *Godey's Lady's Book*, a magazine to which her grandmother subscribed. Its glamorous fashion pictures were a delight to a girl who would always love pretty clothes. All of these young Maud

The Lake of Shining Waters

Charlottetown

read from cover to cover, though the poets and the novels were forbidden for Sunday reading. Maud's grandparents were strict Presbyterians and believed that on the Sabbath one should behave only in a religious manner by going to church and Sunday school and turning the mind away from frivolous things. But she could read books of sermons and John Bunyan's *Pilgrim's Progress* on Sundays, and a book about Pacific Island missionaries "in which I revelled because it was full of pictures of cannibal chiefs with the most extraordinary hair arrangements."

Chapter 2
The Widening World

Maud's father had been making trips to far-off Saskatchewan, where he eventually settled in the growing town of Prince Albert. Though she had not lived with him since her mother's death, Maud dearly loved her father, saw him often, and missed him sadly when he went to live so far away. But she could write to tell him about the exciting day when the sail ship *Marco Polo* went aground on the Cavendish shore in July 1883, and send him the essay she wrote about it that won third prize for Queen's County in the Canada Prize Competition of 1890. She had seen the famous old ship (a clipper built at Saint John, New Brunswick, and running between Liverpool and Australia) "coming straight on before the northern gale with every stitch of canvas set. She grounded about three hundred yards from the shore and as she struck the crew cut the rigging, and the huge masts went over with a crash that was heard for a mile, above the roaring of the storm." The foreign crew – Irish, English, Scots, Spaniards, Swedes, Dutch, German – with their Norwegian captain, stayed in Cavendish farmhouses for some weeks. Two of the crew were Tahitians, who reminded Maud of the pictures in the missionary book.

Maud could also tell her father when in 1890 she passed her school examinations and took part in an "entertainment" by the pupils, at which she recited and played a piano solo. And better, in August that year she was able to be with him again, when her grandfather, Senator Montgomery, took her on a long journey to Prince Albert. Hugh Montgomery, who

Senator Donald Montgomery

Hugh Montgomery and his second wife, Mary Ann McRae, 1887

had married again and now lived in the West as a government official and real estate agent, felt he was able to offer his daughter a home at last.

To "go West" in those days was an exciting adventure. The last part of the journey had to be made by the Regina and Prince Albert Railway as far as Saskatoon, and from there by other means, probably stage coach. But the great Canadian Pacific Railway was pushing its way rapidly to the west coast, and only three weeks after Maud's arrival the first through train reached the town.

Prince Albert was a boom town. It boasted two bakeries, two hotels, two drugstores, two blacksmiths, two photographers, two jewellers, two breweries; a barber's shop, a millinery establishment, a sash and door factory, three butchers; one gunsmith, one tailor, one taxidermist; two gristmills and three steam sawmills; one brickyard, two printing offices, three purveyors, four painters, five carpenter shops, seven bricklayers and masons; two doctors and a dentist, four law firms and one private bank. "Not a bad showing for a town situated as it has been, three hundred miles from a railway," said the local paper. The North-West Mounted Police division in the town had recently organized a full brass band, and sports were flourishing – lawn tennis, cricket, curling, baseball and lacrosse.

Maud, who was always enchanted by the beautiful scenery, found much in Prince Albert to enjoy. It was not a flat prairie community, but set in a valley 420 metres above sea level, surrounded by forests and lakes and bluffs, and bisected by a satisfactory river where boats plied busily in summer and dog teams sped in winter. And Maud could now see some of the aboriginal people, the romantic "children of nature" she had imagined – alas, they were not then the brave, proud people she had expected, but generally dispirited men and women who walked the streets in poverty and distress.

She also had a new family to get to know; a young stepmother and a new baby, Kate – a little half-sister – to love and cuddle, "the dearest sweetest prettiest little angel you can imagine." There was a new Presbyterian church to attend, new friendships to make in high school. Maud gave recitations at local concerts and church entertainments, had fun tobogganing, enjoyed "the yellowness and mellowness" of a western autumn, was terrified by the ferocity of western thunderstorms. "I positively *crouched*. It seemed as if every simultaneous crash and flash must rend the house in pieces."

That year in the West had its triumphs for Maud Montgomery. It brought the first publication of her writing. For years, ever since she had been able to scribble, she had been writing her own stories: descriptions of her favourite haunts, accounts of visits, biographies of her dolls and her cats.

Young Maud

She had tried poetry, too. She longed to be a great poet like Byron. When she was nine she had shown a short poem to her father, who said it didn't sound like poetry – it didn't rhyme.

"It's blank verse," she protested.

"Very blank," her father replied.

In school in Cavendish she and a friend had scribbled verses on their slates about some of the teachers, when they should have been doing sums. To their horror, the teacher asked to see what they had written, and they only just escaped the embarrassment of being made to read them aloud to the class. Maud had dared to send some of her poems to American and Canadian magazines, but none of them had been published.

In Prince Albert, however, the unbelievable happened. Father came home one night waving the Charlottetown *Patriot*, which had just arrived by mail, and there, on the front page of the issue of November 26, in a full column of print, was Maud's poem – all 39 verses, with her name in large capitals at the bottom – about a Prince Edward Island legend. More success was to follow. In June of the next year, the

Prince Albert *Times* published Maud's article, "A Western Eden," about Prince Albert and Saskatchewan.

Though she found much to enjoy on this visit, Maud missed her beloved Cavendish, and in the summer of 1891 her father took his homesick daughter back to the Island. Homesickness was not the only trouble. Maud had not much liked her stepmother, who was only about ten years older than herself and expected too much household help from her young stepdaughter. Another baby, Bruce, had been born, and Maud resented the babysitting she was required to do. ("The baby is so cross. Oh my! He is a terror. One of us has to have him in our arms the whole time.") The weather was intermittently bad – "cold and rainy all the time, and the mud" – and Maud missed the warmth of close family ties. "It is dreadful to be among strangers all the time."

Her western experience, however, had given Maud much to remember, though she never gave any of her books a western setting. As usual, what had impressed her most were the scenic beauties of the little town "nestling at the foot of the terraced hills...and beyond it the vast sweep to the forest primeval...the level grassy meadows...picturesque bluffs which curve around, every few yards, to enclose a tiny blue lake...the magnificent river that rolls its blue tides freighted with the mysteries of former ages, past its poplar-fringed banks, with the busy little town on the one side and the unbroken forests of the northland on the other."

She expressed her disappointment in what had happened to the aboriginals. She had half expected, she wrote, "to see a dusky warrior, clad in all his ancient panoply of war-paint and feathers, spring from the shadows..." But "the warrior never does appear...he belongs to an extinct species now." Nevertheless, the young author had great hopes for Saskatchewan – a "country where prosperity and freedom are awaiting thousands...Hurrah for Saskatchewan!"

Maud, aged sixteen

Chapter 3
The Years of Waiting

Back in Cavendish, Maud returned to school to prepare for the entrance examination to Prince of Wales College in Charlottetown, where she studied to become a school-teacher. During a year of teaching at Bideford, P.E.I., she never once gave up her hope of becoming a writer. She had sold a poem to an American magazine, and wrote jubilantly, "It is a start, and I mean to keep on. Oh, I wonder if I shall ever be able to do anything worthwhile in the way of writing. It is my dearest ambition." She was too tired to write after a long day in the schoolroom, but she got up at six o'clock, dressed by lamplight, and, wrapped in a heavy coat, with her feet tucked beneath her for warmth, she would write for an hour each morning with frozen fingers in a cold house.

Next winter she went to Halifax, Nova Scotia, and enrolled at Dalhousie College for a special course in English literature. Here she became known as "the girl who writes stories and poems for magazines and gets paid for them." In what she called her "Big Week" she had earned $5 for a juvenile story in a Philadelphia magazine, $5 from the Halifax *Evening Mail* for the best letter on "Which has the greater patience, man or woman?" and $12 for a poem in *Youth's Companion*.

Two more years of teaching in Prince Edward Island followed, first at Belmont Lot 16 and then at Bedeque. Maud never stopped writing, "grinding out stories and verses on days so hot that I feared my very marrow would melt and my gray matter be hopelessly sizzled up. But oh, I love my work! I love spinning stories, and I love to sit by the window of my room and shape some 'airy fairy' fancy into verse." Much of her work was now being published, with useful small cheques coming in from time to time. In March 1898, Grandfather Macneill died, and Maud returned to Cavendish, where her

Maud, aged nineteen

grandmother was now alone.

For the next thirteen years Maud Montgomery lived in Cavendish, until her grandmother's death in March 1911, except for one year, from the fall of 1901 to the summer of 1902. For these months she worked in Halifax as proofreader and writer for the Halifax *Daily Echo*. "I'm a newspaper woman!" she wrote in her journal.

But she kept on writing her poems and stories. She learned to write at odd moments squeezed from a day beset with the noise of machines and loud voices and telephone bells, interrupted by galleys to be proofread, people to be interviewed, small paragraphs to be written for the *Echo* about hat sales, the Easter Parade, October frosts and local weddings. She was now selling her stories and poems to a variety of magazines in Canada and the United States, mostly potboilers with fantastic plots because the editors paid well for this kind of story. Sometimes editors would ask Maud to write a serial, and hint at the kind of plot they wanted. "It is a very sensational yarn," she wrote about one such story in 1906, "written to suit the taste of the journal that ordered it and I don't care much for writing such, but they offer a good price for it. It deals with a lost ruby, a lunatic, an idiot boy, a mysterious turret chamber and a lot of old standard truck like that."

It was all good practice even if she didn't much care for it, and Maud stuck doggedly to the goal she had set herself. Only occasionally at this time did she succeed in writing what she

Cavendish Capes, near the Macneill homestead

most enjoyed, a poem she felt had expressed just what she wanted to say. "I've written one real poem out of my heart," she recorded in a week when potboilers had taken most of her time. Though true writers must always hope for the power to move the hearts of their readers, Maud recognized the limitations of her talent. "I am frankly in literature to make my living out of it," she told a friend. "My prose sells and so I write it, although I prefer writing verse. I know that I can never be a really great writer. My aspiration is limited to this – I want to be a good workman in my chosen profession. I cannot be one of the masters but I hope to attain to a recognized position among the workers of my time." In 1902 she made $500 from her writing. Two years later it was $591. They were big sums for a writer to earn in those years, and Maud Montgomery might be called Canada's first successful freelance writer.

She had enjoyed her year as a newspaper woman, even if the life was a hectic one at times. But she had to go home. Though her Uncle John, on the adjoining farm at Cavendish, worked his father's land too, Maud's grandmother was finding her household tasks too heavy for a woman now nearing 80, and Maud left Halifax to take on part of the responsibility and to keep her grandmother company. She was not altogether unhappy during these years, because she loved Cavendish, and she was still able to enjoy her private visions and her special responses to every scene and every event. One springtime she wrote, "It was like being born again to see the drifts go and the catkin bud on the willows." Another day she wrote about a visit to the seashore. "We had a wild storm of wind and rain the day before but this evening was clear, cold, with an air of marvellous purity. The sunset was lovely beyond words...The woods are human but the sea is of the company of archangels."

But the beauties in which she so much delighted were not enough. She was growing older, and longed for the companionship of a husband, and a home of her own. In her early twenties, when she was teaching in a rural Island school, she had fallen in love with a young farmer whom she felt she could not marry because he was socially and intellectually her inferior. Shortly afterwards, she became engaged to a man she respected, but she broke the engagement because she found she did not love him. By 1906, when she was 32, she no longer had such high expectations. "After all, this is a practical world and marriage must share in its practicalities," she wrote to a friend. "If two people have a mutual affection for each other, don't bore each other, and are reasonably well mated in point of age and social position, I think their prospects of happiness together would be excellent if some of the highest up-flashings of the 'flame divine' are missing."

Maud wrote this way because, secretly, she had become engaged to the Presbyterian minister at Cavendish, a good-looking, well-educated man of 36 named Ewan Macdonald. She was not in love with him, but liked and respected him, and felt sure they could have a happy life together and give each other pleasant companionship and care. They could not hope to marry while Maud's grandmother lived and needed her, and they were not able to see very much of each other in the next few years, because Ewan went to Glasgow for a year to study theology, and then was sent to work in other churches some 40 to 100 kilometres distant from Cavendish.

Ewan Macdonald

Yours very sincerely
E. Macdonald

Chapter 4

The Woman Inside

George Boyd MacMillan

As the years passed, life became less easy for Maud, in spite of the flashes of delight that came to her from the lovely countryside so dear to her heart. "I am sometimes lonely in the house," she wrote, "or when walking with uncongenial company, but I have never known a moment's loneliness in the woods and fields. I have ripe, rich, rare good company there." She often suffered from nervous headaches, which were not helped by "poor old Grandma's set ways of age and rapidly increasing childishness." She was finding, too, that her ideas about religion, so strongly urged on her from childhood according to her grandparents' narrow and unwavering beliefs, were changing.

Maud's grandparents, sternly religious Presbyterians, were strict with their granddaughter, treating her with firm kindness but without much outward show of affection. As a child, Maud had dearly loved them both, but in later life she commented rather bitterly about some of the rigid rules by which she was surrounded. "In many respects," she wrote, "they were unwise in their treatment of me." She remembered, with particular "anger, humiliation and disgust," once being forced by her grandmother to kneel on the floor and pray to God to be forgiven for being a bad girl. It was an invasion of the child's personal privacy and dignity, and it left her with a hatred for prayer and religion that would have horrified her grandmother if she had realized the depth of Maud's resentment.

Yet in this small community she would have shocked her friends and neighbours if she had dared to argue or to disagree with what everyone else so firmly believed. She was fortunate in having two good pen friends, to whom she could write freely without fear of criticism, and express her doubts and her ways of thinking.

Ephraim Weber

One of these was Ephraim Weber, an Alberta homesteader whose German family, Mennonite farmers in Pennsylvania, had come to Canada before he was born. Mr. Weber had not spoken English until he was twelve years old, and greatly envied Maud her childhood of books and reading. At the age of nineteen he had gone back to school with students little more than half his age, to catch up on the education he had missed. He spent some time as a teacher, and then took up a

Maud photographing her beloved ocean

homestead tract near Didsbury, Alberta. In later years he continued his education in university, and went back to teaching, which he never really enjoyed. He was disappointed to find that he could not make his students feel as strongly as he did about the deep pleasures of learning.

Like Weber, Maud's other pen friend, George Boyd MacMillan of Alloa Scotland, carried on an extensive correspondence with "kindred spirits" in many parts of the world, but Maud was probably the person with whom both men exchanged more letters, and for the longest time. The correspondence went on for 40-odd years, and for Maud, whose increasingly busy life became silted up with things that had to be done rather than things she wanted to do, it became an outlet for expressing views and ideas she could not talk over with anyone else.

"Like yourself," she wrote to George MacMillan, who was a journalist on a local Alloa paper, "I have been scribbling all my life. Six years ago I began to inflict my scribblings on a public that suffereth long and is kind. I have gotten on well and make a comfortable living for one small girl by my pen, besides finding a vast deal of pleasure in my work." She described herself for her latest correspondent.

Apart from my literary bent, I am small, said to be very vivacious, and am very fond of fun and good times generally...I am interested in many things and love living. I have a camera and enjoy taking photos...I love fancy-work, CATS, horses, pretty dresses and feminine things generally. Revel in books. Don't go in for athletics but love out-of -doors.

In her early letters, Maud gave MacMillan useful information about markets for writing in North America – what editors wanted, length of articles and stories, payment. She sent him copies of her poems. He returned envelopes "fat with clippings and postcards," and some of the pieces he had written for the Alloa Journal. He too loved the outdoors. He sent her a sprig of heather, shells, bits of rock, flowers which she wore in her hair to a concert. She sent him a maple leaf, a box of red rose leaves. Over the years he sent long and deeply appreciated accounts of holidays spent in various scenic areas of Britain.

With both Weber and MacMillan, Maud carried on animated discussions about literature, about the possibility of life after death, about reincarnation, morals, fairies. Is discontent helpful to development? Do old people take life less seriously than the young? Why does a trivial event often influence a life more strongly that an important one? Surely all beauty contains a spark of the divine? Is sin in the motive or the act? Will we ever be able to carry out our good resolutions?

If our correspondence is to be really a help and inspiration to each other [Maud wrote] *it is necessary above all else that it should be perfectly frank and sincere. We must feel that we are perfectly free to write as we will, without fear of shocking the other by heresy in any views, spiritual or temporal. You may ask me any questions you wish on any subject and I will answer as freely and frankly as there may be light in me to do. Only thus, I think, can a correspondence between people personally unknown be mutually helpful and interesting. In personal intercourse conventional disguises may serve a good and kindly purpose in promoting harmony but I hold them unnecessary in such a friendship as ours.*

Freedom from the necessity of "conventional disguises" in her letters to her pen friends was a godsend to Maud as she found herself less and less able to accept some of the narrow, moralistic viewpoints she had been taught, and questioning some of the basic beliefs of Christianity. What would the good folk of Cavendish have thought had they known their Sunday School teacher thought her class of girls "stupid and commonplace"? She had to "follow the old traditional paths of thought and expression or I would get into hot water immediately." Her friends would probably have been shocked to learn that Maud had little belief "in any particular kind of a future life. I believe that there is life after death, that's all." They would have been scandalized to know that she was wondering whether religion had been a curse or a blessing, and that she said, "I can not accept the divinity of Christ."

She was fast learning the ability to disguise her real feelings – to wear a public face that said nothing of what she felt and thought.

As a rule, I am very careful to be shallow and conventional where depth and originality are wasted. When I get very desperate I retreat into realms of cloudland....I learned that that world and the real world clashed hopelessly and irreconcilably, and I learned to keep them apart so that the former might remain for me unspoiled. I learned to meet other people on their own ground since there seemed to be no meeting place on mine....I found that it was useless to look for kindred souls in the multitude.

At the same time, she was earnestly examining her own character with a view to self-improvement.

The trials of an uncongenial environment should be regarded as discipline....I see now plainly that I needed the training very much and that it has done me much good in many ways but chiefly in enabling me to form habits of self-control....I used always to rush to extremes in any emotion, whether of hatred, affection, ambition, or what not, that came uppermost. It was a very serious defect....But it certainly has been much modified and as a consequence I am a much more comfortable person to others and myself.

Formal Charlottetown portrait of Maud

Her letters showed her to be witty, vivid and alive. But

Lucy Maud Montgomery

Maud also wrote of sick headaches, nervous spells, and the disillusionments that simmered behind her controlled public face. Her rapturous, magic childhood had been diminished by reality, thought it remained alive in the secret places of her heart and would burst out joyfully in the book by which she would be remembered.

Chapter 5
Anne of Green Gables

So, until March 1911 when her grandmother died, Maud Montgomery lived the quiet but busy life of any country housewife, except for her writing. She kept her rebellious thoughts to herself, expressing them only in letters to her pen friends. She taught her Sunday School class, acted as secretary and editor for the Cavendish Literary Society, did the flowers for Sunday services, worked in her garden, baked cakes and entertained members of the family who came to spend summers on the farm. And she kept on writing stories, poems, more stories, more poems, and finally, a book.

Anne of Green Gables had started life as a short serial for a girls' magazine. But as she read through what she had written, Maud began to like her young heroine and thought her story could quite well be extended to book length. She sent the manuscript to five publishers, all of whom promptly returned it. Maud was discouraged. She tossed it into an old hat box in the clothes room and forgot about it. When she came across it some months later while rummaging for something else, she decided to cut it back to its original length and offer it, as she had originally planned, as a serial that might earn a few dollars. However, on reading it over, she thought "it didn't seem so very bad." She decided it was worth sending it out one more time before reworking it. This time, it was accepted, together with a suggestion that she begin right away on a sequel.

"I thought girls in their teens might like it but that was the only audience I hoped to reach," she wrote, astounded at the book's instant success when it was published in June 1908. The little red-headed orphan girl had touched the hearts of all readers. "The most fascinating book of the season," wrote the Montreal *Star*. "An idyllic story, one of the most delightful books we have read for many a day," commented the New

The first page of the manuscript of Anne of Green Gables

York *American.* The venerable 73-year-old author Mark Twain sent a personal letter to Maud. "He wrote me that in Anne I had created 'the dearest, and most lovable child in fiction since the immortal Alice'. Do you think I wasn't proud of Mark's encomium?" Almost the only critical voice was that of the New York *Times*: "Anne is a bore...a mawkish, tiresome, impossible heroine."

In February 1909, Maud received her first royalty cheque for the sum of $1,730. She was well into the sequel demanded by her publishers, which appeared the following year as *Anne of Avonlea.* Altogether, Maud was to write eight books about Anne, and by the time the last one, *Anne of Ingleside,* was written in 1939, she was heartily tired of her heroine. "If the thing takes," she had written prophetically after her second *Anne* book, "they'll want me to write her through college. The idea makes me sick....If I'm to be dragged at Anne's chariot wheels the rest of my life, I'll bitterly repent having 'created' her."

In the first five years of publication by the L.C. Page Co., *Anne of Green Gables* ran through thirty-two printings. In the first three years of publication in England, nine thousand copies were sold. By 1956, three million copies of Montgomery novels were circulating in British countries, not counting Canada, and *Anne of Green Gables* accounted for six hundred thousand of these. Since then, a quarter of a million copies of the *Anne* books have been sold in Britain alone. Since 1954, more than seven million copies have been sold in translation in Japan. As well, there have been translations in more than fifteen other languages and the English edition in Braille.

In 1908, Maud was finding that fame had its disadvantages. Tourists were demanding to meet her, and "I don't want to be met." She resented newspaper publicity about her private life. She was not feeling well, suffering from headaches, lack of appetite and weariness. She was also discovering unexpected jealousies and unfriendliness among her relatives and friends. "A certain class of people will take it as a personal insult to themselves, will belittle you and your accomplishment in every way and will go out of their way to make sure that you are informed of their opinions," she wrote to Ephraim Weber three months after publication of *Anne of Green Gables*. She was kept busy explaining that no, *this* particular character was not a portrait of *that* real person. "You can't describe people *exactly* as they are. The details would be true, the *tout ensemble* utterly false. I have been told my characters are marvellously 'true to life' – nay, Cavendish readers have got them all fitted to real Cavendish people. Yet there isn't a portrait in the book. They are all 'composites.'"

Some of the many translations of L.M. Montgomery's books

Maud in 1908, the year of publication of Anne of Green Gables

There were some pleasures and rewards, however. When the governor general, Earl Grey, visited Charlottetown in 1910, he made a special request to meet the author of *Anne*, and Maud had a delightful time buying the pretty new dresses she loved. Later that year she was invited to spend two weeks in Boston at the home of her publisher, and was entertained at luncheons by literary and patriotic clubs. Here she visited the homes of Emerson, Hawthorne, Thoreau and the Alcotts, and was amused by a placard on a tumble-down house on the Concord road that read: "This is the original house Paul Revere *would* have stopped at if he had ever ridden this way."

Maud's latest book, *The Story Girl*, was completed, though it would not appear until the following summer. It was not about Anne, but about a group of Island children who gathered to hear tales of mystery and ghosts and star-crossed lovers. In this book, which remained Maud's favourite, she was able to draw on her own experiences and on local and family legends. It was published just in time for the warm reviews to make a pleasant wedding gift when she and the Reverend Ewan Macdonald were married on 4 July, 1911. Grandma Macneill had died, aged 86, in the previous March, and Maud began to make a home of her own.

Chapter 6
Mistress of the Manse

In the small village of Leaskdale, Ontario, the people of St. Paul's Presbyterian Church congregation were busy preparing the Manse for their new pastor and his bride. Their quiet, Island-born minister had asked for a three-month leave of absence, as he would be marrying Miss Lucy Maud Montgomery and they wanted a honeymoon abroad. With true Scottish reticence he did not say much about the lady, but admitted, when confronted with a copy of *Anne*, that he understood she was a writer.

They were married in the front room of Uncle John Campbell's Park Corner home, and Maud wore the traditional bridal dress of ivory silk crepe de chine and lace, and a tulle veil with a coronet of orange blossom. That afternoon she and Ewan left for Montreal to board the White Star liner

Park Corner

Ewan and Maud Macdonald on their honeymoon visit to the Glasgow Exhibition, 1911

Megantic.

This trip was an especial joy, enabling Maud "to verify the impressions formed by reading," and now at last, to meet George MacMillan, her pen friend in Alloa. The Macdonalds visited in Scotland the land of Robbie Burns, thinking of *Tam o'Shanter* and *Highland Mary*, and the Sir Walter Scott country, thinking of *The Lady of the Lake*. They saw Abbotsford, Dryburgh, Melrose Abbey. They stopped off in J.M. Barrie country, and drove to Culloden with "a nice old driver who knew all the history and legend of everything."

In mid-August the two Canadian travellers went from Edinburgh to Alloa in Clackmannanshire to meet George MacMillan. With George and a friend , they visited the Glasgow Exhibition, and made a week-long tour from Berwick-upon-Tweed to explore old castles, deserted mills and Flodden Field.

They had visited the land of Ewan's ancestors in the Inner Hebrides. Now, after exploring the English Lake District, they went to find the early home of Maud's grandmother in Suffolk. In London and the surrounding countryside, Maud delighted in the sense of history: the Temple Church, Hampton Court Palace, Shakespeare's Stratford, Stonehenge and Windsor. Though she had revelled in the scenic beauties of Britain, Maud found none "more beautiful than can be seen any evening at home." And in none of her later writing did she use any of the scenes she had visited on her only trip abroad.

Home in Canada again, the Reverend Ewan and Mrs. Macdonald settled down in Leaskdale where they would live for the next fifteen years, until Ewan was "called" to the congregation at Norval, a few kilometres west of Toronto, in

The Manse, Leaskdale

1926. The people of both communities took Maud to their hearts, a little astonished that she seemed like one of themselves. So famous a writer could have been snobbish, haughty and reserved. Instead, people found her warm-hearted and welcoming, from the first moment of meeting at an official church reception, when Maud piled her hair high and greeted them in her wedding dress.

"Leaskdale is a very pretty country place," she told MacMillan, inviting him to visit them (but he never did). "It would be almost as pretty as Cavendish if it had the sea....It is a farming settlement...only fifty miles from Toronto. I find the people here nice and kind. Yes, I like Leaskdale very much. But as yet I do not love it." Norval was "a pretty village in the valley of the River Credit." But neither Leaskdale not Norval could ever quite match, for her, the magic of her Island. After a summer's visit to Cavendish, she wrote: "Oh, I felt that I belonged there – that I had done some violence to my soul when I left it."

Maud took very seriously her role as a minister's wife. Some years later, she wrote of "the leadership which the minister's wife can give, especially in rural communities where it may otherwise be lacking....From my viewpoint, the minister's wife has a special opportunity for service which is a privilege and not a duty." But for Maud Montgomery Macdonald, the duty ranked higher than the privilege. She performed her duty with all her heart, but for most of the time she felt "caught in the 'wheel of things' as Kim says." She was "very busy – too busy. I haven't time to savor life at all."

Her responsibilities increased when her two sons were born, Chester in July 1912 and Stuart in October 1915. (In August 1914 there was a stillborn son, Hugh). Though Maud was fortunate in having capable help in the house, she had to become adept at doing two things at once, sewing while she recited

Chester (above) and Stuart Macdonald (right)

or read to her children; working out plots and dialogue for her stories as she drove in the cutter or the buggy drawn by Queen, the smart little black mare, or when she travelled by train, or even as she was dressing (parishioners remember hearing "muttering" sounds from behind her closed door from time to time); crocheting or knitting during meetings and pastoral visits. She took her proper part in every aspect of church life: the pastoral visiting, the

quilting parties and pie socials, the Women's Missionary Society meetings, the Young People's Guild. Teenagers liked her, and her pleasure in reciting and reading found a welcome outlet at their gatherings and in helping them produce and act in plays. Sometimes she wrote papers on subjects that were turning over in her own mind: as early as the mid-1920s she was trying to stir up young Leaskdale minds to understand the idea of atomic energy and other deeply puzzling aspects of the universe.

Through all the years in this busy round, Maud managed to keep a couple of hours daily for writing. In 1912 and 1913, she published *Chronicles of Avonlea* and *The Golden Road*, both collections of short stories , and in

Ewan Macdonald and the boys at Leaskdale

1916, T*he Watchman & Other Poems*. Poetry was always her first love, though she never succeeded in expressing with real inspiration the beauty she longed to capture. "She did her writing early in the morning," her son Stuart remembers, "and reading late at night....She read and reread all the classic English literature, and with a fabulous memory, could quote most of Shakespeare, Wordsworth, Byron and all the famous

L.M. Montgomery, 1922

English poets, but also read all the current books, magazines and newspapers, and ate up one or two detective novels daily." In letters to MacMillan and Weber, she frequently discussed the books she was reading at the time.

"People have a nice feeling about the Macdonalds," a friend says. The nice feeling was well earned. Ewan did his best to be a good minister, preached short down-to-earth sermons, was jovial and hearty. The people liked him for his dedication to his work, his rather bluff manner that made him seem one of themselves. But the congregation never realized, as Maud soon did, the great depths of depression into which Ewan could sink, and which became an ever increasing burden she had to bear. She kept a cheerful face and wrote to friends about his ill health – his "nervous prostration," his insomnia, his low spirits – as if these were the ordinary ills most people suffer from time to time. But only at the end of her life did she reveal the true weight of that burden. "My husband is very miserable. I have tried to keep the secret of his melancholic attacks for twenty years, as people do not want a minister who is known as such."

Chapter 7
War Years

The horrors of World War I were a dreadful drain on Maud's mental and physical health. She was far from the battles and though she had many friends and relatives engaged in the fighting, no one very close to her was in danger. But a person as sensitive and imaginative as Maud could conjure up the frightful scenes of frontline fighting almost as easily as if she had personally experienced them, and the fate she saw for the world, if Germany won, was a source of constant fear. She wrote to MacMillan:

Oh, is it not hideous – unbelievable – unthinkable!...Oh, surely, surely, Germany cannot win! It is no joke but a simple fact that I have not had one decent dinner since the war began. Our dinner hour is one. The mail comes in at 12.30. If the news is good it excites me, if it is bad it upsets me and I can eat little. While if I decide to exert all my will-power and refuse to look at the papers until after dinner the suspense is worst of all and I can eat absolutely nothing. When I tell this to our comfortable, stolid country people who, from a combination of ignorance and lack of imagination do not seem to realize the war at all, they laugh as if they thought I was trying to be funny. Those who perceive that I am in earnest think I am crazy.

The "comfortable, stolid country people" learned, later in the war, from hard personal experience, to share Maud's fears and sorrows. "In Uxbridge, our little market town seven miles away, a regiment is billeted for the winter," she wrote to Weber, "and about seventeen of our finest boys have enlisted right here in our little rural community. Our church on Sunday is full of khaki uniforms, and oh, the faces of the poor mothers! The church is full of stifled sobs as my husband prays for the boys at the front and in training."

She filled "every available chink and cranny of time" with sewing and knitting for the Red Cross (she was president of the local branch) and with helping to pack huge bales of supplies. To add to her misery, the birth of her third child Stuart had been followed by a series of illnesses that ended in anemia and loss of energy, and Ewan had a six-week bout of bronchitis. The war news continued to be all bad. "I shall never forget the agony of those two weeks when it seemed likely that the Germans were going to smash their way through! It was just when everything here was at its worst – E's illness and my own breakdown. I couldn't eat or sleep. I grew old in that fortnight."

It was probably to be expected that a person so passionately concerned about what was happening would begin to find meanings in her dreams, and to believe that these were sent to give her knowledge, or warning, of what was about to happen.

In one dream, for instance, a frightful storm arose, from which a khaki-clad soldier had rushed into the manse for refuge, upon which the skies suddenly cleared and Maud found herself crowned with flowers. "You may smile," she told MacMillan, "but in the terrible weeks of the Verdun offensive that dream was really my only comfort."

Another "storm" dream seemed to forecast the attack on Rumania.

I dreamed that I was in the old sitting room down home with some friends. Suddenly we noticed a gloom, and running to the window I saw that exactly half the sky from the horizon to the zenith was covered with a dense black pall which seemed to have risen up in a moment. As I looked , one livid, jagged bolt of lightning rent it asunder. We all ran to do various things as a preparation for the storm – shutting doors, closing shutters, driving in chickens etc. Then when everything was done we discovered that there was no longer any storm to prepare for – the sky was clear, the sun shining. I woke at once with the conviction that another German offensive was coming but from what quarter I could not imagine. When the attack on Rumania began I never doubted that Bucharest would fall – I believed that was what the bolt of lightning foretokened. Assuredly the first half of my dream came true.

At every crisis she had spent sleepless nights. Until she

heard that Jutland had been a victory and not a defeat, "I walked the floor like a lunatic." The shelling of Paris gave her a night that seemed "an endless agony." During the long-drawn-out Verdun offensive, she had felt "as if I were slowly bleeding to death."

The living room at the Macneill farmhouse

Despite the tremendous tensions, the daily routine of home and church and writing had to go on. Out-of-town trips for business, for duty and for pleasure, made inroads on her time. Maud was now in constant demand for speaking engagements, to give readings from her own work. Her need to go back to Cavendish to refresh her spirit in its beauty was not satisfied as often as she wished during these years, but in 1918 she did manage to spend six weeks in Prince Edward Island during the summer. She had never dared before to do more than gaze at her old home from the outside. This time she found the courage to enter the house.

It was a sad sight. The old maple grove was gone and most of the old birches. How sorrowful, how forlorn the old house looked.

I slipped around to the back and saw that the door was secured only by a wire easily unfastened. I did what I never expected to do again -- I opened the door and once more crossed the old threshold. I stood in the old kitchen. It was quite clearly visible in the dusk. A damp odor of decaying plaster hung heavy on the air. I went through the sitting room and the parlor. In each I shut my eyes and thought myself back into the past. Everything was around me as of old – each picture, each chair, each book or flower in its old place. I went up the dark stairs. I stood on the threshold of my old room where I had written my books long ago. But I did not go in. The window was boarded up and the room was as dark as midnight.

As long as she lived, Maud would need the Island to renew her spirit. But such happiness made her apprehensive. "The gods do not give such gifts out of mere wantonness of giving. They are meant as consolation prizes for the dark days to follow." She left the Island after this visit with the feeling that never again would it be so delightful. But in the summer of 1927, she spent "a blissful month....I have never been away. And oh, how lovely – and lovelier – and loveliest – it was. How satisfying." She rejoiced to find herself once again on buggy rides, just poking along, in no hurry to get anywhere, "past little hollows full of scented fern, past little 'pole' gates under spruce trees, past stone dykes hung with wild strawberries, and over looping blue rivers and through valleys where amber brooks called – and always the fragrance of dead fir coming unexpectedly every little while – that fragrance which is as the wine of old romance to me and always opens some floodgate in my soul."

Chapter 8
The Public Face

When she had been a young teacher at Bideford on the Island, Maud had sent to a Toronto magazine a sample of her handwriting for character analysis. "You are of a rather domineering disposition," she was told, "but knowing how to master yourself as well as others, are very controlled. You are very fond of elegance and luxury, of aristocratic manners, etc. *You know how to suppress and hide your internal thoughts and feelings to such an extent as to appear utterly different from what you really are.* You can be extremely amiable, affable and obliging. You have a will of your own. You like comfort and ease. You are very economical, very politic and diplomatic, suspicious and distrustful. I can tell you a great many more things from your very interesting handwriting."

A sample of Maud's handwriting

When Maud sent these line to MacMillan she underlined the sentence printed in italics. She had always been conscious that the duties and appearance of conformity required by her position as minister's wife were often at variance with her innermost thoughts and beliefs. She, who was not a mixer – "I hate the word" – had had to become a mixer, or at least "an excellent imitator of one." She told of the time in 1920, when "as a sort of duty" she had sat up late at a young farmer's wedding reception. "I had to sit there till two in the morning and talk to scores of the women who were sitting in rows around

Maud Macdonald in evening dress

the room, until I felt like a machine that just talked ever on without any volition. My head ached, my back ached, my mind and soul ached." She listened patiently to chatter about hens, eggs, new babies, the high cost of living "and all the other entrancing subjects of 'conversation' which prevail hereabouts – at least when 'the minister's wife' is present." She suspected that when the minister's wife was absent, the people would talk "racy and malicious and *interesting* gossip, and enjoy themselves much better, but alas, ministers' wives dare not meddle with gossip, else would their tenure in the land be short and troubled."

Ministers' wives, she found, had to be careful to conceal other emotions too. "What agonies I have endured betimes when I was dying to laugh but dared not because I was the minister's wife."

But none of those among whom she lived were ever allowed to know the boredom Maud suffered so often, the weariness she felt when church duties took her from the things she really wanted to do. Some of the demands on her time were due to her role as a popular author, and these she undertook willingly, though she was often as bothered by them as by the endless demands of church work. Looking back over 1921, when she had visited Montreal and Cleveland, among other places, to give readings, and had worked to help the Canadian Book Week campaign, she wrote, "I've just tore about and cussed!"

Anyone in public life must, on many occasions, meet people about whom they know little and care less, and take part in events they do not enjoy. If Maud sometimes pretended interest where she felt none, this was done out of courtesy and good manners, not to deceive. A perceptive Leaskdale friend remembers travelling with her by train to a nearby town and being gently requested to forgive her silence: she liked to use the time for thinking out some tricky scene in her current book. "Yet, when acquaintances chanced to board the train and join us with a lot of chatter, no one would ever have guessed, from Mrs. Macdonald's manner, how unwelcome their intrusion must have been."

She was saved from complete despair by her ability to live

The family on holiday in Kentucky, 1924

an inner life of mind and spirit, in a land of things-as-they-should-be. "Whatever real life I have lived has been in the realm of the spirit."

Maud did not, in fact, entirely dislike what she sometimes deplored. About the endless round of missionary meetings, ladies' aids, Women's Institutes, Sunday School teachers' meetings she wrote:

Sometimes I get so sick of them that I could hang myself on the handiest gooseberry bush rather than go to another. And yet – it's odd – it's always in prospect only that I hate them. When I get to them I find myself really quite enjoying them. I like 'making things go', having, so I have been told, a 'gift' that way. It is really only because of the inroads they make on my time that I rise up and howl occasionally.

Yet she could write at another time, "I have lost the art of living entirely....It isn't right. We weren't meant to live like that." Separately, she could have enjoyed any of the activities she was involved in. All together, crammed into one life, they were too much.

To most observers, Maud appeared to be "a woman of personal charm and winsomeness, as broad-minded and practical as she is imaginative, with a keen sense of humor, happy in the keeping of her home and the interests of the parish...a mother who mothers her children personally...(who) does her own housekeeping with the skill and despatch of a woman trained to it."

Maud's younger son Stuart wrote of his mother, "She was extremely sensitive, although an excellent dissembler, and though she experienced great peaks, she also fell to great depths emotionally, which does not make for tranquillity. This rigidity and sensitivity prevented any easy camaraderie in the family, but she was capable of inspiring deep affection in all of us."

There were many great peaks of happiness in her life. Delight in her sons runs through all her letters as she writes of their baby chatter, the pillow-fights at bedtime, the Hallowe'en nights when the little boys were "dancing in wild abandon round a jacky-lantern on the gatepost and shrieking like tortured savages," and of Stuart's teenage triumph as junior gymnastic champion of Ontario (he became national champion in 1933). The success of *Anne of Green Gables* brought her many honours, from the invitation to meet Canada's governor general, Earl Grey, in 1910, to a meeting with Britain's prime minister, Stanley Baldwin, when he visited

Lucy Maud Montgomery in her garden

Ottawa in 1927 for Canada's 60th anniversary. Another British prime minister, Ramsay MacDonald, told of his disappointment on missing Prince Edward Island during a tour of Canada – he had always wanted to see the Island since reading L.M. Montgomery's books.

"Oh, you read her books?" he was asked.

"Yes....I've read every Montgomery book I could get my hands on two and three times over."

In 1923, Maud was invited to become a Fellow of the Royal Society of Arts in England, the first Canadian woman to be so honoured. In 1935, she was invested with the order of the British Empire. Her own progress up the long room at Rideau Hall in Ottawa to curtsey to the governor general and receive the medal went off "nicely," but she was amused by the gorgeous lady in the elegant dark blue dress who proceeded up the room unaware that her white underslip was showing.

Another delight in her life was her great love of cats. "How dreadful it would be not to love a cat!" she wrote to MacMillan. She was never without a cat, and mourned them in deep sorrow when they died. "I wonder if all the spirits of all the pussy folk I have loved will meet me with purrs of gladness at the pearly gates?"

Maud in a field of PEI flowers

The Public Face

Chapter 9
Viewpoints and Opinions

When she was a little girl, Maud had been repelled by a visiting Bible Society traveller. A thin, pale man with a straggly beard and squeaky voice much disliked by Maud, he asked her, "Little girl, isn't it nice to be a Christian?" Remembering his "shivery bony form, pinched blue face, purple hands" as he hunched over a fire on a frosty night, Maud associated her dislike for him with a dislike for what she felt must be his form of Christianity. This, together with her grandmother's narrow views, started her thinking in her own way about what religion should be – something beautiful, something that would free the spirit, not confine it. When she married a minister, it was therefore all the more difficult for her to hold ideas more than a little different from those her husband was preaching.

As a young woman she had written, "I call myself a Christian in that I believe in Christ's teachings and do my poor best to live up to them. I am a member of the church believing that with all its mistakes and weakness it is the greatest power for good in the world and I shall always do what I can to help its cause." When, in 1926, the United Church of Canada had been formed from some of the Presbyterian congregations joining with the Methodists and Congregationalists, Maud was not happy. "A too big church is not a good thing. It becomes clumsy and unwieldy....It is no use to say that people want a church for a 'social community centre"....If Jesus of Nazareth is shelved, then the church will crumble, for he was her 'one foundation' in whatever sense you take it." Maud thought the church had made many mistakes in the past. "Personally, I really believe the day of the church is done...but – a tree that took 2000 years to grow will be a long time a-dying, and I think both United and Continuing and all other churches will function for centuries yet before they finally 'peter out'."

Though she sat decorously in the pew each Sunday, attended church meetings, church socials, church bazaars, taught in Sunday School, Maud could write, "I don't number public prayers as necessary. I don't care for any kind of public prayers, not even in church. These are nearly always farces, and generally unpleasing farces." Maud was much more likely to find her spiritual inspiration from the great outdoors. Like her Anne, "If I really wanted to pray...I'd go out into a great big field all alone or into the deep, deep woods, and I'd look up into the sky...into that lovely blue sky that looks as if there was no end to its blueness. And then I'd just *feel* a prayer."

When her son Stuart, seven years old, was learning his catechism, he came to the question *Why did God make all things?* The answer was *For His own glory.* Indignant Maud thought the answer seemed to be "an abominable libel on God." She told Stuart: "That is not how the question should be answered. God made all things for the love and pleasure of creating them – of doing good work – of bringing beauty into existence."

The beauty of the world was indeed Maud's source of inspiration. With Anne, she could cry, "Spring is singing in my blood...I'm seeing visions and dreaming dreams." When she was in her mid-fifties, when she was "so tired I didn't want to go on living," she went outside just before preparing for bed, and experienced "one of the rare splendid moments" of her life, hearing the wind sing "in the garden of the wild gods up on the hill called 'Russell's pines' by prosaic people. *Some* Spirit moved there – my soul caught its call and stood mute and rapt as in some vast temple of the night."

Her quick mind was always probing for answers to the mysteries of the universe. With George MacMillan she shared a great interest in the stars. "I think astronomy much the most fascinating study in the world," she wrote, and she used to go out on dark nights with a pair of field glasses to look at the skies. "Half the time I don't know whether I'm on 'the good red earth' or roaming the Milky Way...I feel as if I had literally been millions of miles away and that all my ordinary surroundings were strange and forgotten." She was sure there must be life on other planets. "It would be absurd to think God would waste so many good suns."

As early as the 1920s, Maud was thinking about the future of science in the world.

We are, I believe, entering on an age of wonderful scientific development. We will do things that are hardly dreamed of as yet but we will not write great literature or paint great pictures. We can't have everything at the same time. We will fly round the world – and solve the secret of the atom, but there will be no Shakespeares or Homers. They went out with the gods.

In 1927 she wrote, "The discovery of a way to release the energy of the atom will be the next epochal thing after the dynamic of Jesus." But two years later she wrote that there would still be some things hidden. "God will always keep a few secrets to himself."

Matthew, played by George Merner, and Anne (Malorie-Ann Spiller) in a scene from the musical Anne of Green Gables *staged for the Charlottetown Festival*

Because of her own eager search for knowledge, Maud had little patience with young people who were uninterested in education. She did not approve of the Ontario law that made students stay in school until they were sixteen. "I don't believe this universal 'education' of everybody is the blessing in practice that it is in theory. To me much of the 'education' of today is like an inadequate spoonful of wine in a glassful of water." When Ephraim Weber, trying hard to arouse the interest of his students, grew pessimistic, Maud wrote encouragingly, "Why worry because one jug hold a quart and another only a pint. And that most receptacles are sieves, holding nothing at all. Be wise. Just keep on pouring, since pour you have to – and be thankful you have something to pour."

But she did not think the young people of the day – or of any day – were very much different from those in the past. "I can honestly say that I see no difference between the boys and girls of Leaskdale and the boys and girls I mingled with in my teens. Some of them are stupid and silly and crass. So were some thirty years ago." To reporters who continually demanded to know "What is your opinion of girls of this so-called fast age?" Maud replied, "Just as good as those of any other generation....Girls are freer to express themselves now. The pressure is off, that is about all the difference there is."

The concept of reincarnation, the rebirth of the soul in a new body, had great appeal for Maud.

That idea of the immortality of character *never appealed to me. Too few of our characters would* bear *immortality. I would* like *to believe in a personal immortality but find it difficult. I* do *believe that the spark of life within us we call the spirit is immortal and indestructible and that when it is released by the decay of the body it joins again the great tide of life that flows through the universe until its next 'incarnation' – which happens, I believe, whenever some fit organism seizes it and holds it. And so on in unending cycles. But I can't believe as I would like to that it retains aught of our memories and personalities.*

She wrote to Weber: "What a strange thing this death is....If we listened to Nature's teachings we should be happier, truly believing (I hold) that death is simply a falling asleep, probably with awakening to some happy and useful existence."

Chapter 10

Busy Author

Through all the years of this involved life, Maud managed to keep a couple of hours each day for her writing. The success of the first two Anne books brought demands from her publishers for further sequels, and though even the second book about Anne had bored her, Maud obediently set to work to produce new Anne stories.

Tracy Ann Moore as Anne Shirley in 1986 production of the musical

After *Rilla of Ingleside* (the story of Anne's daughter) had appeared in 1921, the sixth book about "that detestable Anne," Maud wrote, "I am sick of her and wonder that the public isn't too." But the public wasn't sick of Anne, and in 1936 and 1939 two more Anne books appeared, *Anne of Windy Poplars* and *Anne of Ingleside*, both written by their author without much pleasure in her work, though readers found them as lively as ever.

In 1919, Maud saw the first filmed version of *Anne of Green Gables* and did not like it. The star, Mary Miles Minter, "was not my gingery Anne,"

The Manse at Norval

the scenery was not right for Prince Edward Island, nor was the American flag. Moreover, when she had signed the contract for the book, film rights were not thought of, and it was ruled that these did not belong to her, but to the publisher. As a result, Maud received nothing for this and a later film, a "talkie." After the second film, the actress who played Anne (Maud liked this one) changed her acting name from Dawn O'Day to Anne Shirley.

When a contract was offered for a film of *Anne of Windy Poplars* in 1939, Maud had learned her lesson. She "signed five contracts, each in 19 different places – ninety-five times in all!"

She had also had other trouble with her publishers, the L.C. Page Co. of Boston. Her original contract had given them the right of refusal of all books she might write for the next five years, and she had become dissatisfied with her treatment by the firm. After she had severed her connection with them, they decided to publish some of her early stories. "Be not deceived," she wrote to Weber. "It is a collection of old short stories which they held for years under the old contract but would never publish so long as they could get anything better." She had agreed to their publication, but with certain deletions to avoid any mention of Anne (as agreed in her contract with her new publishers). Page, however, printed them in their original form, without her authorization, and they appeared in 1920 under the title *Further Chronicles of Avonlea*. This began a troublesome lawsuit that was not concluded until nine years later. The case went through the courts of two states and up to the Supreme Court of the United States before it was decided in Maud's favour.

In October 1921, Maud was telling her pen friends that she had "a new kind of heroine," and liked her. She had begun work on *Emily of New Moon*, which she dedicated to George MacMillan. Many reviewers wrote that it was her best book since *Anne of Green Gables*. Two more Emily books were published, *Emily Climbs* and *Emily's Quest*, and some readers liked them better than the Anne books.

"People were never right in saying I was Anne," wrote Maud, "but in some respects they will be right if they write me down as Emily." Emily's life story follows Maud's life closely. Emily wrote letters to her dead father just as Maud used to write to her own dead mother. Emily remembered seeing her beautiful mother lying in her coffin, and Maud always thought she remembered seeing her own mother, too, though she was so very young at the time – not quite two years old – that her memory may have been simply the picture her mind's eye saw when someone else told her about it. Both Emily and Maud were brought up by an elderly and rather strict relative. Emily invented a private language, just as Maud did, to tease some of her school friends. Emily had a typewriter that, like Maud's, made the capital letters very faint and wouldn't print the letter *m* at all. Emily, like Maud, was proud of her family history and her ancestry.

Maud saw her new heroine as so different and so fresh that she was disturbed when Ephraim Weber did not agree with her. "You say 'Of course Emily is another Anne'. Well, she may be, but if so I have entirely failed in my attempt to 'get her across' to my readers." Emily's background of family and tradition, she felt, was very different from "the hail-fellow-well-met little orphan from nowhere." She could not see any resemblance "except one or two superficial ones in the stage

Lucy Maud in 1922

they walk on."

Anne and Emily do, in fact, share many similarities. Both are orphans, both are vividly imaginative, both are passionate in their responses. Both are in the care of guardians and required to behave in ways that often do not match their own reasonable wishes. Adult requirements often seem to both children to be unfair, and they deeply resent unfairness. Most of the adults in Emily's world are relatives. In Anne's world they are more often neighbours. But in both worlds, the adults have similar personalities – loving or severe, crusty or peculiar, forthright or withdrawn.

Maud was amused to read that in Weber's opinion the only overdrawn character in *Emily of New Moon* was the teacher, Mr. Carpenter, whom she had taken from real life. Readers almost always reacted the same way, she had found: they tended to fit the wholly invented characters to real people, and were sure that those drawn from real life were the imaginary ones.

Her writing is sometimes overcoloured and sentimental, but Maud redeems herself by a delicate sense of humour and a real ability to understand the children of whom she writes. She was often able to catch the oddities of character – and sometimes gently ridicule them – in a single pithy sentence. Aunt Frances, refusing to take the aspirin that would have relieved her headache and "still enduring God's will in her bedroom." James Baxter, who had stopped talking to his wife "and *nobody knows why*." Systematic Luke Elliot, who marked on a chart every New Year's Day "all the days he means to get drunk on – *and sticks to it*." Aunt Wellington, "who always enunciated commonplaces as if uttering profound and important truths." No wonder young and old world over delightedly recognized some of the quirks and mannerisms of their friends and associates in the figures of Maud's fictional world.

In February 1926 there had been the big upheaval of the move to Norval after fifteen years in Leaskdale. "Roots that have been rooted as long as that are not pulled up without pain," she wrote. But once settled, Maud entered into community life with all her old vigour and interest. She was now the author of fourteen books, and had been working on the fifteenth, *The Blue Castle*, which she intended for adult readers, though she described it as "merely an amusing (I hope) little comedy." This book, published in August 1926, she dedicated to Ephraim Weber, and the scene was set not in Prince Edward Island but in Muskoka, Ontario, where she had spent a happy holiday.

At the end of 1927, Maud found herself more than ever trapped on the "Wheel of Things." She had plunged at once into her church work, and that winter had "had some pleasure and a great deal of worry training a group of young people to give a play." Norval friends remember her work with delight. "Those plays she put on were a tremendous hit everywhere. The group used to give a performance at several different places – in church basements, school halls – and the proceeds would be split between the Norval group and the host community." From the first year's performance they made $500.

Maud really needed a secretary, but was sure she could not find one who would consent to live in such a quiet little spot as Norval. The next few years followed the usual pattern of rush, worry and illnesses. In 1929, three weeks of influenza had been followed by a fall down some stairs and a sprained arm for seven weeks; for three of them her arm was in a sling. December brought a bad cold, January intestinal flu and a mysterious rash on her face, February tonsillitis. She was feeling, she said, like a demoralized dish-rag.

Magic for Marigold was published in 1929, and *A Tangled Web* in 1931. And there was always mail to answer. From the beginning she had heard from "men and women who are grandparents, boys at school and college, old pioneers in the Australian bush, missionaries in China, monks in remote monasteries, and red-haired girls all over the world." Sometimes the letters arrived in bundles and basketsful. "She maintained a voluminous correspondence," says her son, "writing by hand every fan letter reply." In the fall of 1931 she had her first experience of broadcasting when she read a couple of poems over the air, but she missed a live audience. The novelty of radio had hit her first in 1923, but with apprehension rather than with pleasure. "These discoveries treading on each other's heels give me a sense of weariness and *homesickness* for the slower years of old....Those of us living now had to speed on with the willy-nilly....And none of these things really 'save time.' They only fill it more breathlessly full."

The winter of 1933/34 was a terrible one, perhaps to pay for the mild one the year before. There was unbroken cold from early November until early March. Maud was beset by colds and the ceaseless effort to keep warm. Ewan had gone through influenza and insomnia to a complete breakdown, with nearly four months in a sanatorium, two more months at home in misery, and a month of recuperation on the Island. It was, Maud wrote, "quite the most terrible year I have ever lived." No wonder that she "staged a little breakdown of my own and for six weeks couldn't sleep or eat or work."

Nevertheless she had carried on courageously. *Pat of Silver Bush* (with a heroine "like Anne," she wrote) was published in 1933, to be followed in 1935 by *Mistress Pat*. This year Ewan retired from the ministry, and in July 1936, Maud was writing from "Journey's End" in Toronto, "on a winding road on the banks of the Humber River." The house backed onto a deep ravine where pines, oaks, bracken and wild flowers delighted her. She was charmed to discover that the wind howled around the house in storms. And she was happy that both boys, now at university, could live at home again.

Lucy Maud Montgomery in 1935

L. M. Montgomery

Chapter 11
End and Beginning

In 1936, the Canadian government proposed developing a national park in Prince Edward Island to be centred on Maud's beloved Cavendish, which would celebrate all the places precious to her – Lovers' Lane, the Lake of Shining Waters, the Dryad's Bubble – and with a house to represent Green Gables furnished as nearly as possible to fit the descriptions in Maud's book. At first she thought it was "sacrilege" to throw open to possible desecration by the public "all those lanes and woods-encircled fields where I roved for years....They will never – can never be the same to me again." Sensibly, however, she recognized that the government action had saved the area from being broken up and sold to individual and possibly uncaring owners, who might cut down the trees and destroy the lanes. "Now they are to be preserved exactly as they are."

Lovers' Lane, Cavendish

The L.M. Montgomery

When she visited the area in 1939, she felt quite happy about the project. All her beloved haunts had been maintained, and new beauties added. Down a flight of stone steps she was charmed to find a cup hung on a birch tree for all who would drink from the water of the Dryad's Bubble, now surrounded by a stone wall.

A new heroine, to join Anne and Emily and Pat, had made her appearance in *Jane of Lantern Hill*, published in 1937. The story was set partly in Toronto, but chiefly in Prince Edward Island. In September 1938, Maud started on what would be the last *Anne* book, and completed it in four months of hand writing. This was *Anne of Ingleside*, about the baby days of Anne's children, and it was published in 1939. Maud had not written the *Anne* books in the chronological sequence of Anne's life, which made the work harder and more tiresome for her. She had expected each book to be the last, and had to

L.M. Montgomery Macdonald

fill in the gaps when publishers demanded yet another *Anne* book.

In these last years of the 1930s, Maud had suffered many setbacks. She was worried by domestic problems – "worry over many things, some of them the kind that can't be told to the world but must be hidden and not spoken of." Ewan's health had continued to deteriorate. "It was more than nerves this time," she told MacMillan in 1937. "For about two months in the summer he was a mental case, and among other symptoms lost his memory completely." She faced the problem bravely, as always. "I could not bear to have him go to any institution for I knew no one could understand him as I did, for I have nursed him through so many of these attacks."

As a result of worrying, and following a bad attack of influenza in the winter of 1937/38, Maud herself had a nervous breakdown. She was obsessed by a dreadful restlessness – "for four months I lived in a sort of hell on earth" – walking the floor to try to gain control of her nerves. It was four more months before autumn brought relief, and at last, in the spring of 1939, she found herself better than she had felt for years.

But she was on a downhill path. The outbreak of World War II had further depressed her already low spirits. "It is not *fair* that we who went through all this before should have to go through it again." The enormous waste and tragedy of war, added to her husband's worsening mental health, bowed her down. Fortunately, neither of her sons was immediately threatened. Chester had escaped military service because of shortsightedness, and Stuart, still a medical student, was not allowed by the Medical Council to leave until his course was completed. Maud tried to continue her writing, working on what she had hoped to publish as a sequel to *Jane of Lantern Hill*, but it was never completed. In mid-1940, she had another "dreadful nervous breakdown" after a bad fall and the depressing war news.

In 1941, her long letters to her friends had dwindled to a few postcards. "I am no better....I have had a very bad year....We have lived to see beauty vanish from the world....You do not know the blows that have fallen on my life for years. I tried to hide them from my friends...." To MacMillan she wrote: "I thank God for our long and beautiful friendship. Perhaps in some other incarnation in some other happier world we will renew it....May God bless you and keep you for many years. There are few things in my life I have prized as much as your friendship and letters."

Maud Montgomery Macdonald died on April 24, 1942. Perhaps at this time she was glad to lay down a life that had become too full of burdens. Her sons and her husband accompanied her body to the Island where her spirit had always been, for burial in the little Cavendish cemetery. Nearly two years later, she would be joined by Ewan, who died in December 1943. For her memorial service "a great concourse of people" thronged the Presbyterian church or stood outside, on a day of windy sunshine, with snow still holding in patches and gulf ice visible in the distance. Some birds had returned already – wild geese, a few songbirds. The minister who had performed her marriage, the Reverend John Stirling, presided at her funeral. *The Watchman*, her poem about the Resurrection, was read, as well as extracts from *Chronicles of Avonlea*.

Among the important and distinguished names in Island history, said the Reverend Dr. Frank Baird, who represented the Moderator of the General Assembly of the Presbyterian Church in Canada at the funeral, "I do not think any will outshine the star that shone, and will continue to shine down through the ages in Lucy Maud Montgomery Macdonald....the distinguished authoress robed 'in the white majesty of death' here before us today."

Without doubt Maud had suffered much weariness in her life as the wife of a minister, and the need to keep silent about many of her beliefs. But of course there had been compensations. "I look back and see many lovely things....Houses that always seemed pleased to have you come to them. Frank, ungrudging tributes, appreciative, priceless words that cast a sudden rainbow over existence. Dear gentle souls who never once made me feel that I had said the wrong thing....Little friendly, neighborly offerings now and then – the jar of cream or jelly, the box of eggs, the root of an admired perennial. ....And the dear, dear women I have known!"

In March 1931, she had written to MacMillan: "I say to myself 'I believe in a series of re-incarnations. If that is true I am really nearing the time when I will be young again.'"

Today the lively musical based on *Anne of Green Gables* is the foundation for an annual festival in Charlottetown, and thousands of tourists flock every year to see Anne's house and the beloved red roads of the Island. Thousands of children the world around delight afresh in Anne and Emily and Pat and Jane and the dozens of dearly loved characters with whom Maud peopled her stories. L.M. Montgomery needs no monument of stone when such a living one endures.

Tourists visiting the Green Gables house outside Charlottetown

Further Reading

Eggleston, Wilfrid. *The Green Gables Letters.* Toronto: Ryerson Press, 1960.

_____. *While I Still Remember.* Toronto: Ryerson Press, 1968.

Gillen, Mollie. *The Wheel of Things.* Toronto: Fitzhenry & Whiteside, 1975.

McCabe, Kevin, ed. *The Lucy Maud Montgomery Album.* Markham: Fitzhenry & Whiteside, 1999.

_____. *The Poetry of Lucy Maud Montgomery.* Markham: Fitzhenry & Whiteside, 1999.

Montgomery, L.M. *The Alpine Path.* Toronto: Fitzhenry & Whiteside, 1974.

Lucy Maud Montgomery, The Island's Lady of Stories. Prince Edward Island: The Women's Institute, 1963.

Ridley, Hilda. *L.M. Montgomery.* Toronto: Ryerson Press, 1956.

The "Anne" series, arranged in chronological order of Anne's life:

Anne of Green Gables: Anne's childhood
Anne of Avonlea: Anne as teacher.
Anne of the Island: Anne goes to college.
Anne of Windy Poplars: Letters to her boyfriend Gilbert Blythe.
Anne's House of Dreams: Marriage and first child.
Anne of Ingleside: Birth of five more children.
Rainbow Valley: The children grow up.
Rilla of Ingleside: Anne's daughter.

Credits

Canadian National 59
Charlottetown Festival 49, 51
Ian Gillen 9
Dr. Stuart Macdonald 5, 7, 13, 17, 19, 25, 26, 28, 30, 36, 39, 42, 43, 45, 52, 55, 63
Kevin McCabe 31
Public Archives of Canada 8(C66939)
Public Archives of PEI 10, 11, 46
Edith Smith 57
University of Guelph Library 4, 6, 12, 14, 16, 20, 21, 22, 32, 33, 34, 35, 36, 58, 60

Index